HANDS-ON HISTORY

PROJECTS ABOUT
The Plains Indians
Marian Broida

BENCHMARK BOOKS

MARSHALL CAVENDISH
NEW YORK

Acknowledgments

Thanks to the following individuals and groups for their assistance: Polly Chase, extension agent for 4H and youth, Fort Berthold Extension Office; Calvin Grinnell, resource development specialist, Three Affiliated Tribes; James Haug, reference librarian, Anthropology Library, Smithsonian Institution; Ione Quigley, cultural resource management specialist, Sinte Gleska University; staff at the George Gustav Heye Resource Center of the National Museum of the American Indian; Robert Taber, chairman, Southern Cheyenne and Arapaho tribes of Oklahoma; Gordon Yellowman, cultural liaison, Southern Cheyenne and Arapaho tribes of Oklahoma. And for help in testing the activities, thanks to Lynne Ravatt of View Ridge Elementary and the fifth grade classes of 2002, Shaina Andres, and Beatrice Misher.

The excerpt on page 16 is based on stories from George Bird Grinnell's *The Cheyenne Indians: Their History and Ways of Life* and *When Buffalo Ran*.

Benchmark Books
Marshall Cavendish
99 White Plains Road
Tarrytown, NY 10591-9001
www.marshallcavendish.com

Text copyright © 2004 by Marshall Cavendish Corporation
Illustrations copyright © 2004 by Marshall Cavendish Corporation

Library of Congress Cataloging-in-Publication Data

Broida, Marian.
  Projects about the Plains Indians / by Marian Broida.
    v. cm. — (Hands-on history)
Includes bibliographical references and index.
Contents: Journey to the past — Where the Plains Indians lived — The
Cheyenne — The Lakota — The Hidatsa.

ISBN 0-7614-1601-3

  1. Indians of North America—Great Plains—Juvenile literature. 2.
Indian craft—Juvenile literature. [1. Indians of North America—Great
Plains. 2. Indian craft.] I. Title. II. Series.

E78.G73B76 2004
978.004'9752—dc21
2002155873

Illustrations and map by Rodica Prato
Series design by Sonia Chaghatzbanian

Copyright for all photographs belong to the photographer or agency credited, unless specified otherwise.

Corbis: 6, 35, Tom Bean/Corbis: 8, Bettmann/Corbis: 15, Historical Picture Archive/Corbis: 16, Sam Kleinman/Corbis: 42 • Getty Images/Hulton Archive: 4, 11, 21, 32-33 • North Wind Picture Archives: 1, 34, 40

Printed in China

1 3 5 6 4 2

Contents

❧

The official name for the buffalo is American bison. Plains Indians depended on buffalo for tipi covers, food, clothing, and tools.

1

Journey to the Past

Listen. Can you hear a **herd** of **buffalo** thundering across the vast grasslands of the **Great Plains**? Do you feel the summer wind, so hot and dry it makes your eyes sting? Do you see a circle of **tipis** on an icy night, lit up like lamps from the warm fires within?

In this book you will journey to the past. You will visit American Indians of the Great Plains at different times during the past two hundred years. The Great Plains is an area east of the Rocky Mountains, stretching from Texas to Canada. You will be visiting the ancestors of the American Indians who continue to live there today.

Two hundred years ago, Indian children did not go to a school. They learned by watching and playing and listening to stories. On your visits to the past, you will do the same. You will make a play tipi, play a game, make a food called pemmican, stitch a pouch, dry a squash, and more. You will learn some traditions of three Plains tribes: the Cheyenne, the Lakota, and the Hidatsa.

I hope you enjoy your travels to the past. As the Lakota people say, *Tan yan waciyanke* (tan yan wa-CHEE-yan-KAY)—"good to see you!"

Nomadic Plains tribes, such as the Cheyenne, lived in tipis year-round. The Hidatsa and other farming tribes lived in tipis only when hunting buffalo and lived in villages of earth lodges the rest of the year.

Here's how to pronounce some Plains Indians tribal names:

Arapaho (uh-RAP-uh-hoh)	**Kiowa** (KY-uh-wuh)
Arikara (uh-RICK-uh-rah)	**Lakota** (la-KOH-ta)
Assiniboin (as-SIN-i-boin)	**Mandan** (MAN-dan)
Blackfoot (BLACK-foot)	**Missouri** (miz-ZOO-ree)
Cheyenne (shy-AN)	**Omaha** (OH-muh-hah)
Comanche (kuh-MAN-chee)	**Osage** (OH-sayj)
Crow (CROH)	**Oto** (OH-TOH)
Dakota (da-KOH-ta)	**Pawnee** (paw-NEE)
Gros Ventre (GROH vahnt)	**Plains Apache** (plains a-PATCH-ee)
Hidatsa (hee-DOT-sa)	**Ponca** (PAHNG-kuh)
Iowa (I-oh-ah)	**Wichita** (WITCH-it-taw)
Kansa (KAN-zuh)	**Yankton** (YANG-tun)

Sometimes tribes have two names, the name they call themselves and the name that someone else (another tribe or white people) has given them. For example, the Dakota people are sometimes called Santee Sioux, or just Sioux. The name *Sioux* comes from their traditional enemies the Ojibwa. (The Ojibwa themselves are often called the Chippewa.) Most Indian people prefer their tribe's own name for themselves.

Where the Plains Indians Lived

This map shows where many Plains tribes lived and hunted 150 to 200 years ago. Tribes in **red** lived in portable homes, called tipis, year-round. They moved from place to place, following the buffalo. Tribes in **blue** were farmers who lived in houses called **earth lodges** most of the year and in tipis only when hunting buffalo.

The United States government forced the Plains Indians on to **reservations** about 150 years ago. Today, many American Indians still live on reservations, but others live in cities and suburbs across the country. Modern Indians wear blue jeans, eat pizza, and play video games like other Americans. Many also go to traditional Indian gatherings called **powwows,** where crafts are on display and where they can take part in their heritage through traditional songs, dances, storytelling, and foods.

An earth lodge

8

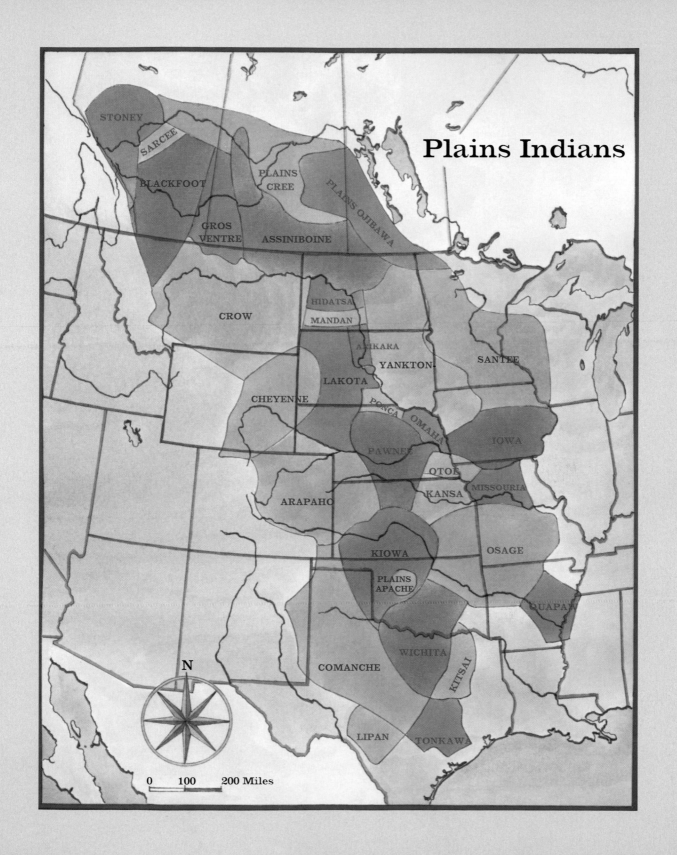

Plains Indians

STONEY
SARCEE
BLACKFOOT
PLAINS CREE
GROS VENTRE
ASSINIBOINE
PLAINS OJIBAWA
CROW
HIDATSA
MANDAN
ARIKARA
YANKTON
SANTEE
LAKOTA
CHEYENNE
PONCA
OMAHA
PAWNEE
IOWA
OTOE
KANSA
MISSOURIA
ARAPAHO
KIOWA
OSAGE
PLAINS APACHE
QUAPAW
WICHITA
COMANCHE
KITSAI
LIPAN
TONKAWA

N

0   100   200 Miles

General George Armstrong Custer and the men of the U. S. 7th Cavalry were defeated by the Sioux and Cheyenne Indians at the Battle of Little Bighorn.

2
The Cheyenne

The Cheyenne were **nomadic**, which means they moved from place to place. They followed the buffalo, hunting them on horseback. The Cheyenne lived in tipis that could be set up or taken down by women in a short time. These tipis were decorated with designs often seen in dreams. This way of life was common to most Plains tribes that followed the buffalo.

The Cheyenne's way of life began to change in the 1830s and 1840s when the United States government claimed lands in the West. Buffalo hunters killed the buffalo that were needed by the Cheyenne. In 1867 the Cheyenne were moved to Indian territory in Oklahoma. Years later, the northern Cheyenne settled on a Montana reservation. Today, Cheyenne continue many of their ancestors' traditions.

Play Tipi

The year is 1888. A Cheyenne girl leads you to her family tipi. "My mother prepared twelve buffalo **hides** to make this. See how soft it is?" the girl asks. "My father painted the designs on the outside. Those are animals he saw in a dream."

    She runs to a circle of two-foot-high tipis. "Here's the play tipi I made," she says. "My friends and I play taking our tipis down and putting them up again, like our mothers do when we move camp." She smiles shyly. "Why don't you make a play tipi? Then you can play camp, too."

You will need:	manila file folder	pencil	markers or paints
	dinner plate	scissors	Scotch tape

1. Open the folder, and lay it flat on the table. Lay the upper half of the plate on top of the folder, as shown. Trace around the plate with a pencil.

2. Cut out the half circle you just made.

3. Shut the half circle. Cut a little square from the corner, about ½ inch wide.

4. To make the door, keep the half circle folded. Find the straight edge that is NOT along the fold. Now find the end of this edge opposite the cutout square. Near that end, cut a half circle about the size of a walnut half. Save the pieces for smoke flaps.

5. Open the large half circle.

6. Make smoke flaps. Tape a small half circle to each side of the square you cut out, so the round parts stick out, as shown.

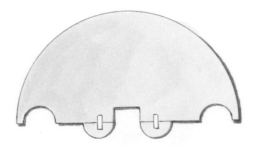

7. Decorate the outside of the tipi (on the side without the tape) by painting symbols of things that are important to you. Use markers or paint.

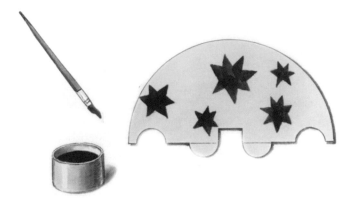

8. Make some folds from the top of the tipi to the bottom, like spokes in a wheel.

9. Bring the two halves of the door together to make a cone.

10. Tape the tipi closed without overlapping the edges.

11. Fold out the smoke flaps at the top.

Strong winds could blow smoke from the tipi fire back inside. Two smoke flaps near the tipi's top kept this from happening.

The Cheyenne hunted buffalo on foot before the Spanish brought horses to the Americas.

Uses for Buffalo Parts

It's 1845. A group of Cheyenne men return from hunting buffalo, leading packhorses loaded with meat and hides. Among them ride a thirteen-year-old boy, with a bow and arrows, and his father. When they arrive at their tipi, the boy's father says, "My son, I will honor your success by giving a gift to an elder, in the way of our people." Then he shouts, "My son killed his first buffalo today—a calf! To celebrate, I will give Red Wolf a good horse." An old man in tattered clothing, Red Wolf, approaches their tipi. He mounts the horse and rides around the camp singing about the boy's success.

Column A lists some buffalo parts. Column B lists how the Cheyenne used them. Match the part with its use, writing your answers on a separate sheet of paper.

Column A: Parts

1. horns

2. bones

3. hide (two answers)

4. meat

5. stomach, bladder, or membrane from heart

6. sinew (strong, stringy tendon that joins muscle to bone)

7. brains

Column B: Uses

A. scraped and dried hard to make moccasin soles, packing cases, and shields

B. softened in mouth and used as sewing thread or strings for bows

C. eaten fresh or dried to make **jerky** and pemmican

D. mixed with liver and fat and rubbed into hides to soften them

E. cut and sharpened to make knives, **awls** for sewing, and other tools

F. boiled until soft, shaped around a rock, and cut into bowls, dippers, and spoons

G. scraped, dried, and softened to make tipi covers, winter robes, bedding, and moccasin tops

H. dried and used as cooking pot or bucket

Moccasin Game

It's 1840. In a crowded Cheyenne tipi, you watch six men play a moccasin game. One team of three men sits opposite the other three. Between the two teams are two moccasins. Excitement sizzles in the air. One of the men is quickly passing his hands over the moccasins. The other team watches closely. A man on the first team beats a drum rapidly to distract them, his voice rising and falling in a special moccasin game song. Suddenly a man on the second team points at the first man. Everyone shouts and laughs as the first man shows two small sticks—one in his hand, the other in a moccasin.

A boy near you whispers in your ear, "They might play all night long. If it gets too hot in here, come outside and I'll teach you how to play."

You will need:

- at least two people
- two small sticks, pebbles, or other objects you can hide in your hands
- two moccasins or shoes
- pencil and paper to keep score
- drum (optional)

---

1. Form two teams. Decide which one will hide the sticks first. Choose one person on that team to be the first hider and one on the other team to be the first guesser.

2. Make up a special song for the game. The hider's team can sing, shout, or beat a drum to distract the guesser.

3. Announce the beginning of the game.

4. If you are the hider, you can hide the two sticks one of these ways:
   - **one in each hand**
   - **one in each moccasin**
   - **one in your RIGHT hand and the other in the LEFT moccasin, or**
   - **one in your LEFT hand, and the other in the RIGHT moccasin.**

   These are the ONLY choices.

5. Move your hands a lot as you hide the sticks. Try to confuse the guesser. Say when you are ready for him or her to guess.

6. If you are the guesser, show your guess one of these ways:

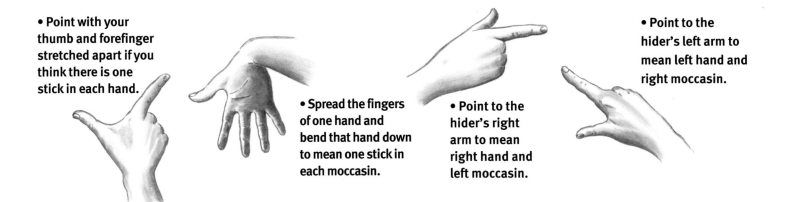

• Point with your thumb and forefinger stretched apart if you think there is one stick in each hand.

• Spread the fingers of one hand and bend that hand down to mean one stick in each moccasin.

• Point to the hider's right arm to mean right hand and left moccasin.

• Point to the hider's left arm to mean left hand and right moccasin.

7. A correct guess means a point for your team. Your team gets to hide the sticks next. Guessing wrong means a point for the other team. They get to hide the sticks again. Take turns with your teammates being hider and guesser.

8. If someone hides a stick in a hand and a moccasin on the same side, score a point for the other team.

9. Play until one team wins four times in a row.

A chief and his squaw travel across the Great Plains with all of their belongings loaded onto a travois. Before Plains Indians had horses, dogs pulled lighter loads on smaller travois.

3

The Lakota

According to Lakota legend, their first home was beneath the Black Hills of South Dakota. The Lakota call the Black Hills "the heart of everything that is."

Long ago, the Lakota had no horses. Like other Plains tribes, they used dogs to pull their belongings on sleds called **travois** (tra-VOYZ). After the Spanish brought horses to America, the Lakota could pull bigger loads.

In 1868 the United States set aside the Great Sioux Reservation, which covered much of South Dakota and parts of other states. In 1874 gold was discovered in the Black Hills, and three years later the United States reclaimed part of the reservation—the most sacred part. The army was sent in 1876 to force the Lakota to settle down and become farmers. Many battles followed. One by one, many Lakota chiefs surrendered in 1877, and their tribes were placed on reservations. More Lakota fled to a reservation after Sitting Bull was murdered in 1890.

Today, Lakota live on six reservations in South Dakota. Many work to keep their customs, religion, and language alive.

Model Travois

It's 1860. A group of Lakota families prepares to move camp. Two women are harnessing a pair of tipi poles to a horse. Tied between the poles is a platform made from willow **saplings**, or young trees.

"That's a travois," a Lakota boy tells you. "My mother and aunt will tie things onto the platform for the horse to pull."

The boy's mother is attaching a large upside-down basket onto the platform, making a cage. "What's that for?" you ask.

The boy grins. "My little sisters," he says. "They are too young to ride a horse, so they ride on the travois. If it tips over, the cage will keep them safe."

You will need:

- small brown paper bag
- scissors
- water
- 8–10 brown or tan pipe cleaners, 12 inches long
- 2 sticks or pieces of thin dowel two to three times longer than the horse
- 2 smaller sticks, about 6 or 7 inches long
- thin cardboard, about 6 x 8 inches, from cereal box or backing to a notepad
- Scotch tape
- plastic horse, 5–12 inches long from nose to tail

1. From the paper bag, cut a piece twice the size of your hand. Crumple it and wet it, then let it dry flat.

2. Cut two pipe-cleaners into quarters. Cross the long sticks or dowels near one end. Fasten with two pipe-cleaner quarters, as shown.

3. To make the platform, choose the longer of the two sticks you have left. Use two or more pipe-cleaner quarters to attach it to each of the two poles.

4. Attach the last stick an inch or so above the other short stick.

5. To finish your platform, cut a pipe cleaner into quarters. Lay each piece crosswise across the two smaller sticks, and fasten both ends.

6. Now make a bundle of buffalo hides. Roll the cardboard into a tube that fits neatly on your travois platform. (Trim if necessary.) Tape closed. Wrap with the paper you moistened, then tie with a pipe cleaner. Attach it to the platform with two more pipe cleaners.

7. Pass the last pipe cleaner around the horse's neck or chest, and attach both ends to the upper end of the travois, opposite the platform.

Model Shield

It's 1810. A Lakota grandfather is helping his fourteen-year-old grandson make his first shield. The boy is stretching buffalo hide over a round wooden frame.

"On the front, I will paint the vision I saw last summer," says the boy. "It will protect me in battle."

"Always remember what it means to own a shield," says the grandfather. "It means you are ready to defend your family and your people. Someday, when you have been brave in battle, maybe you will hang eagle feathers from your shield. The eagle flies higher than other birds and has a higher place of honor. Now, because you are young, you will use the feathers of a hawk."

You will need:

- sturdy white paper plate (such as Chinet brand), dinner-sized
- pencil
- markers
- ruler
- scissors
- cardboard from cereal box or backing to notepad, longer than plate is wide
- stapler
- a one-hole punch
- 3–4 feathers from craft store
- double-stick tape
- 1 package embroidery thread from sewing or craft store

1. Think for a while about the things that give you courage or hope, or that make you feel strong: maybe the sun or an animal. Sketch them in pencil on the back of the paper plate. Then color with markers.

2. Cut a strip of cardboard about an inch wide and an inch or so longer than the width of the plate. Staple it to the rim in two places so that it goes across the front of the plate (back of the shield) and it bows out.

3. Punch 3 or 4 holes around the shield's bottom edge.

4. Cover the shaft of a feather with double-stick tape. Then, starting near the feathery part, wind most of a 16-inch strand of embroidery thread neatly around and around so it covers the spot completely. Tie the end of the thread through one of the holes in your shield. Repeat for each feather.

Making Pemmican

It's 1810. A group of Lakota boys are playing in the late summer heat. Nearby, a group of women are pounding food with stone hammers. You watch as they crush dried buffalo meat and dried chokecherries, pits and all.

"They are making **wasna**," says one of the boys. "Some people call it pemmican. It is good food for wintertime or traveling. It keeps for years." Together, you watch the women add melted buffalo fat and bone **marrow**, and shape the mixture into lumps. When the women look away, your friend darts over, snatches a piece, and pops it into his mouth.

"Yum!" he says, running back. "Want one?"

> ### You will need:
> - 1/3 cup dried cranberries (can use a sweetened kind, such as Craisins) or other dried fruit
> - 1/4 cup (about 1 ounce) beef jerky
> - 2 tablespoons peanut butter
> - knife
> - measuring cups and spoons
> - blender
> - spoon
> - bowl
> - plate or cutting board
> - plastic wrap

This recipe uses beef jerky and peanut butter instead of buffalo meat, fat, and bone marrow.

1. Ask an adult for help.

1. Cut the jerky into 1-inch strips.

2. With a measuring cup, measure the cranberries.

3. Leaving the blender unplugged, add the jerky and cranberries to the blender.

4. Cover the blender and plug it in. Blend the jerky and the cranberries until they are shredded.

5. Unplug the blender.

6. With a spoon, scoop the mixture out into a bowl.

7. Measure out the peanut butter with a measuring spoon, and add to the bowl. Mix with the spoon.

8. Shape the mixture into several 2-inch lumps.

9. Wrap them in plastic wrap, put them on a plate or cutting board, and store them in the refrigerator until you are ready to eat them.

Felt Pouch

It's 1985. A young Lakota girl stitches a pouch. "My grandmother showed me how," she says. "In the old days, they used to sew pouches from buffalo hide and clothes from deerskin. That was before my grandmother was born. She says it is a lot easier to use felt, like I'm doing."

She stitches for a while, then points to some beads in a cup. "I'm going to sew those on the front. My grandmother's teaching me some Lakota designs. Every design has a special meaning," she says. "Do you want to make a pouch?"

You will need:

- tapestry needle (large needle with blunt point and big eye)
- piece of felt, 4 x 12 inches
- 2–4 safety or straight pins
- yarn
- scissors
- 6 or more pony beads (plastic beads, about 1/4-inch wide, available in craft stores)

1. Make sure the tapestry needle pokes easily through the felt. Some felt is too stiff.

2. Fold over about 4 inches of the felt, as shown. Pin it in place.

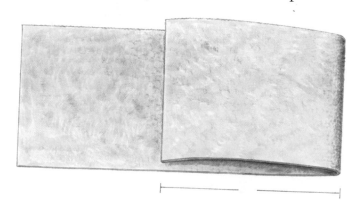

3. Tie a knot at one end of a piece of yarn, and thread the needle with the other end. Starting at the fold, stitch up one side of the pouch through both thicknesses of felt. Use a stitch that wraps around the side of the pouch, so you always push the needle the same way (up or down) through the felt. (See illustration.)

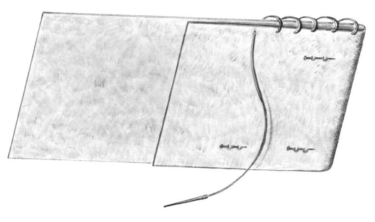

4. At the top of the upper piece, push the needle under one of your last stitches. Do not pull the yarn all the way through. Instead stick the needle through the loop you just made and pull it tight to make a knot. (If it unravels, try again. This time stick the needle through the loop going the other direction.)

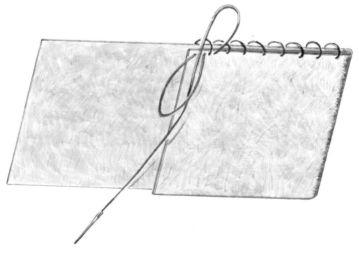

5. Cut off the extra yarn.

6. Repeat on the other side with a new piece of yarn. You now have a pouch. Remove your pins. Fold the top over the front to make a flap.

7. Stitch beads on the front flap. Start at the underside of the felt. Knot the yarn at one end. Push the needle up through the flap, through one to three beads, and back down through the flap. Repeat if you like until you run out of beads. Tie a knot at the end, as in step 3. [Note: Be careful not to sew the flap closed!]

8. To make a carrying strap, stitch a long piece of yarn through the upper fold from underneath. Leave a long enough loop to go over your shoulder. Push the needle back through the fold from above, and knot underneath.

This illustration shows men and women from the following tribes in traditional dress around the year 1800. From left to right, they are Iroquois, Assiniboin, Crow, Pawnee, Assiniboin in gala dress, Dakota man and Dakota woman. These tribes, except the Iroquois, lived on the Plains.

A village of earth lodges

4

The Hidatsa

Like other village tribes near the Missouri River, the Hidatsa once were farmers as well as buffalo hunters. Most of the year they lived in villages of earth lodges. When they went on buffalo hunts, they lived in tipis.

Smallpox, a disease brought by white people, changed their lives forever. Many Hidatsa villages were left nearly empty. The Hidatsa who survived joined with another tribe, the Mandan. Today the Hidatsa, Mandan, and Arikara tribes share a reservation in North Dakota. Together they are called the Three **Affiliated** Tribes.

The bull-boat allowed Indians to navigate shallow waters, small rivers, and streams.

Bull-boat

It's 1869. You are in a bull-boat—a round boat of buffalo hide stretched over a frame of saplings. Kneeling beside you, a Hidatsa woman steers with a wooden paddle. Firewood for the village fills most of the boat.

"My grandmother taught me to build this boat," she says. "She owns a bundle of sacred objects passed down in the family. Only people who own such a bundle may build a bull-boat, or teach others how to build one. The boat must be made according to the sacred ways of our people, with special prayers and songs to keep it safe."

The boat is nearing the village. You hop out and help remove the firewood. The woman straps the boat to her back to carry it home.

You will need:

- brown or tan 12-inch pipe cleaners
- large brown paper bag
- plate or pot lid, about 8 inches across
- pencil
- scissors
- water
- stapler
- Elmer's glue
- cardboard backing from notepad

1. Make a circle with one pipe cleaner. Fasten the ends together. Cut the other pipe cleaners in half.

2. Fasten two halves next to each other on one side of the circle. Fasten their other ends across the circle. Push into a bowl shape.

3. Fasten the other two halves at one end of the circle. Weave them across the first two halves—going under one pipe cleaner and over the next, or over one pipe cleaner and under the next. Fasten them across the circle. Try to keep the sharp ends pointing inside the circle. The woven pipe cleaners should form a bowl.

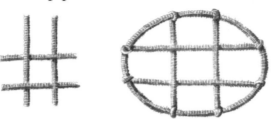

4. Trace around the plate onto the bag, and cut out the circle. (Save the scraps.) Crumple the paper circle, and wet it. Uncrumple it, and set the pipe-cleaner frame you just made on top of it.

5. Wrap the paper around the boat frame, folding the extra paper over the top. Staple in place all around the top pipe cleaner, the one you first made into a circle. Use lots of staples. It is OK to stretch the paper a little. Trim off the extra paper.

6. Repair small tears by gluing on a paper scrap. Big tears require starting with new paper.

7. Finally, cut out a cardboard paddle shaped like a flat shovel.

Drying Squash

It's 1850. A Hidatsa woman cuts squash for drying. "This knife was my mother's," she says, slicing neat rings. "She died from smallpox fifteen winters ago. When I use the knife, I think of her."

She points to the squash slices. "Help me spear these on sticks," she says. "When they are dry, we will string them on cords. In the winter we will cook them and give thanks that we are alive."

You will need:

- winter squash (**Delicata** squash is easiest to slice)
- large sharp knife
- cutting board
- paper towels
- cookie sheet
- oven
- fork
- pot holders
- clean cord or string, about 18 inches long

1. Ask an adult for permission and help.

2. Preheat the oven to 120–150 degrees Fahrenheit if possible. Otherwise set it as low as you can, and leave the door slightly open.

3. Wash and dry the squash. Slice it into circles about 1/4-inch thick on a cutting board. Push out the middle of each slice, with the seeds.

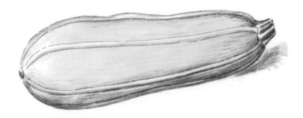

4. Lay two to three paper towels on a cookie sheet. Place the squash rings on the paper towels. Keep the rings separated.

5. In the oven, dry the slices for about six hours until brittle. Open the oven door now and then to let moisture escape. Every hour or so, turn the pieces over with a fork. (Use a pot holder to hold the cookie sheet.)

6. String the squash rings on a cord, and tie into a loop with a strong knot. Hang it in a cool, dry place for days or months.

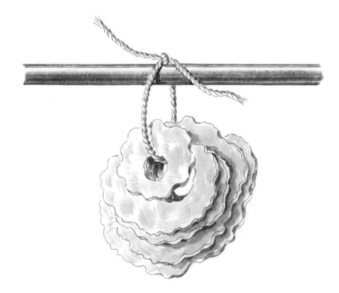

7. To use the squash, cut the cord. Soak the slices in a few cups of water for about 20 minutes. Then boil them until soft, or add to soup.

The Hidatsa were primarily farmers.

Growing a Sunflower

It's 2002. You are visiting the reservation of the Hidatsa, Mandan, and Arikara tribes in North Dakota. A woman is kneeling in a garden plot surrounded by children of all three tribes. She is showing them how to plant corn, beans, squash, and sunflowers. She tells the children that their "great–great–great–great–great–grandmothers planted the same kinds of seeds."

You will need:

- package of dwarf sunflower seeds with instructions
- a one-gallon ice-cream container, clean and dry
- old plate or aluminum pie plate
- handful of pebbles
- potting soil
- watering can or container
- sunny outdoor spot (like a deck or doorstep)
- 3-foot-long dowel or straight stick
- large nail or sharp scissors

If you do not have a garden, plant a sunflower in a container. Plant in spring or summer, depending on the climate you live in. In the fall, eat the seeds!

1. Check the seed package for the best time of year to plant.

2. With an adult's help, poke three to five holes in the bottom of the container. Place the container on a plate. Add pebbles on the bottom, then pack with soil, stopping 1–2 inches from the top.

Some types of sunflowers can grow as tall as 10 feet!

3. Poke a hole in the dirt about 1½ inches deep, or follow directions on the package. Put in a seed and cover with soil. Plant two more seeds about an inch from the first. Water and place the container in a sunny spot. Water once a day.

4. After a few days, watch for sprouts. After a few weeks, pull out all the plants except one. Over the next three months, that plant will grow tall with large flowers. If the plant starts to tip over, insert the dowel or stick in the pot and fasten it to the stem with twist ties. You will know the seeds are nearly ready when the petals fall off. Cut off the flowers, and dry them inside for about four days, until you can pull out the seeds easily.

5. To eat, just remove the black-and-white husks.

Roasting Sunflower Seeds

For a nuttier flavor, roast your sunflower seeds. With an adult's permission, preheat the oven to 350 °F (175 °C). Meanwhile, boil the seeds about 15 minutes, husks and all. Drain them on paper towels. Then spread them thinly on a cookie sheet and sprinkle with salt. Roast them for about 20 minutes, stirring now and then with a wooden spoon. Remove from the oven, and let cool on a rack. When they are cool, pull off the husks and enjoy!

Glossary

affiliated: To be joined.

awls: Tools used to poke holes for sewing.

buffalo: Large, shaggy wild oxen, native to North America, officially called North American bison or *Bison bison*.

delicata: A type of long thin, striped winter squash.

earth lodges: Houses with wooden frames covered with either sod or loose earth.

herd: A group of animals that travel or live together.

hides: The skins of animals.

Great Plains: An area of North American grasslands east of the Rocky Mountains that stretches from the Saskatchewan River in Canada in the north to central Texas in the south.

jerky: Dried meat.

marrow: The greasy, reddish material inside some bones.

nomadic: Moving from place to place.

pemmican: A mixture of dried bison meat, dried wild fruit, and fat.

powwows: Gatherings of different American Indian tribes celebrating their heritage.

reservations: Pieces of land set aside by the United States government for American Indians to live on.

Index

Page numbers in **boldface** are illustrations.

About the Author

Marian Broida has a special interest in hands-on history for children. Growing up near George Washington's home in Mount Vernon, Virginia, Ms. Broida spent much of her childhood pretending she lived in colonial America. In addition to children's activity books, she writes books for adults on health care topics and occasionally works as a nurse. Ms. Broida lives in Seattle, Washington.